SQUEEZE MY LEMON

A Collection of
Classic Blues Lyrics

Written and
Compiled by

Randy Poe

Foreword by

BB King

Cover photo:
Peter Amft

HAL•LEONARD®
CORPORATION

Also by Randy Poe

Music Publishing:
A Songwriter's Guide

Published by Hal Leonard Corporation
7777 West Bluemound Road
P.O. Box 13819
Milwaukee, WI 53213, USA

Trade Book Division Editorial Offices:
151 West 46th Street, 8th Floor
New York, NY 10036

Visit Hal Leonard online at **www.halleonard.com**

Library of Congress Control Number: 2003108574

Printed in Canada
First Edition

10 9 8 7 6 5 4 3 2 1

**You can squeeze my lemon
'til the juice runs down my leg.**

—Robert Johnson,
   "Traveling Riverside Blues"

For **me, the blues began in the** cotton **fields of** Mississippi. Fifty years later, I can still remember hearing my daddy and my Uncle Jack out there singing while they worked. No matter how far away they were from where I was plowing or picking cotton, I could always hear their voices. They sang about whatever was on their minds. They sang from their hearts.

I didn't have a radio back in those days, but my Aunt Mima had a crank-up Victrola. She showed me how to put a 78-rpm record on the turntable, set the needle down, and listen to someone like Blind Lemon Jefferson singing the blues.

I'd put Blind Lemon's "Mosquito Moan" on and listen while he sang, "These gallinippers bites too hard/I stepped back in my kitchen and they're springin' up in my backyard." In the South, we knew all about gallinippers—they were these giant mosquitoes—so I understood what he was singing about.

Aunt Mima also had records by Lonnie Johnson, Bessie Smith, Ma Rainey—all performers who sang from the heart. I could really feel Ma Rainey's hurt when she sang, "I'm so blue, so blue, I don't know what to do." I could also feel her anger when she sang, "I'm gonna find me a pistol just as long as I am tall . . . I'm gonna kill my man and catch the Cannonball."

The blues is a feeling. You can feel the Blues when you hear someone playing the guitar. But when that person starts singing about the bad things that's happened, or why he's so happy, or why he's going to Chicago or Kansas City, then you get a more complete picture of what the blues is all about.

What this book shows you is that the blues can be sad sometimes, but it can be pretty funny, too. Some of it sounds like poetry to me. And some of it would cause a lot of church folks to put their hands over their ears.

On the following pages are words from Robert Johnson, Willie Dixon, Muddy Waters, Billie Holiday, T-Bone Walker, and a lot more. You'll even find some by B.B. King!

Like I said before, the blues is a feeling—and I have the feeling you're going to enjoy these blues.

– B. B. King

When I was 13 years old, I discovered the music of B.B. King. Growing up in the South in the 1950s and '60s, I'd certainly heard his name. I'd even seen it on the marquees of places I was too young to enter. But it wasn't until I heard him singing "The Thrill Is Gone" on the radio in 1969 that I was compelled to take action. After sufficient begging, I convinced my parents to give me a ride to the local record store so I could buy King's album *Completely Well*, which included that incredible song.

Listening to the nine songs on that LP—"Confessin' The Blues," "Key To My Kingdom," "What Happened" and the rest—started me on a journey into the world of blues music that continues to the present day.

But as great as the music on that album was—specifically the classic guitar work of the man rightfully known as the "King of the Blues"—I found myself becoming more and more immersed in the lyrics of the songs he was singing.

The impact of *Completely Well* led me to buy another blues album, and then another, and another, bringing me to the realization that blues lyrics—as is the case with every other style of song—can run from the alarmingly mundane to the amazingly poetic.

At some point literally thousands of albums later (and with practically no storage space left in my house, I might add), I took a little spiral-bound notebook and began to compile a collection of my favorite blues lines.

After a while, the notebook was full. And upon looking back through it recently, I realized that what I had collected was actually a compilation of some of the saddest, funniest, most profound, most eloquent, and, at times, most suggestive phrases ever put to music.

Musically, the blues has always been relatively constricted. Even though it is the very bedrock of American popular music—jazz, R&B, rock and roll, etc.—it tends to be ignored by radio stations, many major record labels, and the general music-buying population at large. After all, most people prefer to look at the house rather than the foundation it's been built upon.

The beauty of the blues is that the vast majority of its lyrics are written from the heart (or perhaps, on occasion, some other vital organ)—frequently by the person singing them. With very rare exception, the lines collected here were written by men and women speaking directly from their own experiences.

Tin Pan Alley songwriters of the twentieth century had little use for the blues, and with a few rare exceptions we are all better off that they generally chose not to impede upon the genre's territory.

Primarily, what you'll find in this book are short phrases the literary world refers to as couplets. (I suspect most blues artists don't give a damn what they're called.) In the blues idiom, a line is sung, usually followed by the repetition (or near-repetition) of the first line, which is then followed by a rhyming (or, in some cases, near-rhyming) line that concludes the thought. When I was jotting down my favorite blues lyrics, I chose not to constantly write down the repeating line twice. The same rule applies here.

The blues quotes in this book are categorized by topic. Some of the lyrics could have fallen into more than one category, so I chose the one most appropriate via the universally accepted, highly scientific coin-toss method. There are also a few songs that have some lines appearing in one chapter while different lines from that same song will appear in another. I think you'll get the idea.

And, of course, there will be some large-brained musicologists more versed in the field than I who will inevitably feel I've erred unforgivably by excluding some seriously deserving blues works from these pages. In the words of B.B. King, "It's my own fault, baby." On the other hand, let them get their own little spiral-bound notebooks.

Little Walter

Women—
the Good,
the Bad &
the Ugly

Women—the Good, the Bad & the Ugly

As a musical form, the blues is generally kept within the framework of a I-IV-V chord progression. Although the word "blue" is synonymous with the word "melancholy," not all blues songs are depressing or sad. In fact, the feelings expressed in the blues cover the whole range of human emotions.

Not surprisingly, many blues songs are about relationships between men and women. And, despite the fact that females are generally accused of being more sensitive and emotional than men, when it comes to the blues, the men who sing them have an awful lot of emotions of their own to express about the ups and downs of relationships.

For every song that tells the story of a lady with a kind heart, there are plenty more about women who treat their men badly—very badly. From "Kindhearted Woman Blues" to "Alimony Blues" to a song about a "female Frankenstein," here are some classic blues lines about women: the good, the bad and the ugly.

It's a cold-blooded world
When a man has to pawn his shoes.
That's the fix I'm in today—
I swear I've been abused.

(*Alimony Blues*—Eddie L. Vinson/Lou Zito)

Bright lights, big city,
Gone to my baby's head.
I tried to tell the woman
But she don't believe a word I said.

(*Bright Lights, Big City*—Jimmy Reed)

If you've ever been mistreated,
You know just what I'm
    talkin' about.
I worked five long years for
    one woman
And she had the nerve to put me out.

(*Five Long Years*—Eddie Boyd)

She calls me her lover,
Yes, and her beggar too.
Now, ain't you sorry, little girl,
That my new little girl ain't you.

(*Hootie Blues*—Charlie Parker/Jay McShann/
Walter Brown)

Well, I went to the river to jump in.
My baby showed up and said,
"I will tell you when."

   (*I'm Tore Down*—Sonny Thompson)

I got a kindhearted woman,
Do anything in this world for me.
But these evil-hearted women,
Man, they will not let me be.

   (*Kindhearted Woman Blues*—Robert Johnson)

My baby don't stand no foolin',
My babe.
Oh yes, she don't stand no foolin'
When she's hot, there ain't no coolin'
My babe.

(*My Babe*—Willie Dixon)

Well, she's got great big teeth
And they're all out of line.
She's 300 pounds of meat,
And she's my female Frankenstein.

(*Real Ugly Woman*—Jerry Leiber/Mike Stoller)

My mama, she done told me,
Papa done told me, too,
"Son, that gal you're foolin' with,
She ain't no good for you."

(*That's All Right*—Arthur Crudup)

Well, I'm sittin' here waitin'
For her to call me on the phone.
She's been gone twenty-four hours,
And that's twenty-three hours
   too long.

(*Twenty-Four Hours*—Eddie Boyd)

I love to look into my baby's face,
I love to feel her in her silk and lace,
And when she kisses me,
    she can make me shout,
Great God a-mighty,
    when the lights go out!

(*When The Lights Go Out*—Willie Dixon)

Well, I've tried to describe her,
It's hard to start.
I better stop now
Because I've got a weak heart.

(*You Upset Me Baby*—B.B. King/Jules Bihari)

Blind Willie McTell

Blues
All Over
the Map

Blues All Over the Map

The blues was born in the American South.
Starting out as call-and-response field hollers on the plantations of Mississippi, the blues began to evolve as it simultaneously moved to the North—or at least out of the deepest part of the South.

Looking to escape from low-paying farm labor, many blues musicians took to the highway, heading out of the Magnolia State to seek success in Memphis and other urban areas. From the 1920s to the 1940s, the blues found new homes in places like Chicago, Kansas City and Houston. By mid-century, even cities as far west as Los Angeles and San Francisco had developed thriving blues scenes.

As blues singers moved to the cities of the North and West, many took up residence on street corners. When the blues moved from the streets into the nightclubs of such areas as Chicago's South Side, acoustic guitars were replaced by the recently invented electric models so that the music could be heard above the din of the crowd.

And when it came to the songs themselves, performers sang not just about where they had been, but about where they now were—as well as where they were heading next.

Oh, the preacher preached,
The sister turned around,
Yes, the deacon's in the
   corner hollerin',
"Sweet gal, I'm Alabama bound."

(*Alabama Bound*—Huddie Ledbetter)

My first night in Chicago
My friends really treated me fine,
Then overnight they all changed
Like daylight saving time.

(*Chicago Blues*—Lonnie Johnson)

Do you know what it means to miss
   New Orleans
When that's where you left
   your heart?
And there's something more:
   I miss the one I care for
More than I miss New Orleans.

(*Do You Know What It Means To Miss New Orleans?*
— Eddie DeLange/Louis Alter)

I'm like a Mississippi bullfrog
Sittin' on a hollow stump.
I got so many women
I don't know which way to jump.

(*Flip, Flop And Fly*—Charles Calhoun/
Lou Willie Turner)

I'm gonna write a letter,
Telephone every town I know.
If I can't find her in West Helena,
She must be in East Monroe.

(*I Believe I'll Dust My Broom*—Robert Johnson)

I might take a train,
I might take a plane,
But if I have to walk
I'm goin' just the same.
I'm goin' to Kansas City,
Kansas City, here I come.
They got a crazy way of lovin' there
And I'm gonna get me some.

(*Kansas City*—Jerry Leiber/Mike Stoller)

I keep thinkin' 'bout that night
   in Memphis,
I thought I was in heaven.
But I was stumblin' through the
   parking lot
Of an invisible 7-11.

(*My Head's In Mississippi*—Billy F Gibbons/
Dusty Hill/Frank Beard)

If she ever comes back to stay,
There's gonna be another
   brand new day,
Walkin' with my baby
Down by the San Francisco Bay.

(*San Francisco Bay Blues*—Jesse Fuller)

Sister got 'em, daddy got 'em,
Brother got 'em, mama got 'em,
I got 'em.
Woke up this morning,
We had them Statesboro blues.
I looked over in the corner—
Grandma and grandpa had 'em too.

(*Statesboro Blues*—Willie McTell)

Come on,
Baby don't you want to go
Back to that same old place:
Sweet home Chicago.

(*Sweet Home Chicago*—Robert Johnson)

Make Mine
a Double
Entendre

Make Mine a Double Entendre

The folks at **Websters define** a **double entendre** as "an expression capable of two interpretations, one of which often has a risqué connotation." Without question, leading the way in the world of double entendres are the lyrics of the blues.

By the time parents started complaining about rock and roll songs being "dirty" in the mid-1950s, blues lyrics with double meanings had already been around for at least three decades. Even the words "rock" and "roll" were sexual euphemisms first referred to musically in blues songs.

And when it comes to sexual euphemisms, food is clearly the number one choice. Pie, cabbage, bacon, ice cream, blackberries, hot dogs, seafood, and of course, the ever-popular lemon all appear on the blues double entendre menu.

I'm a jockey by trade,
I've rode the fastest horses that run.
If you don't start jumpin'
I will show you how the ridin's done.

(*The Best Jockey In Town*—Traditional)

Some call me Woodcutting Sam,
Some call me Woodcutting Jim,
The last girl I cut wood for,
She wants me back again.

(*Crosscut Saw*—R.G. Ford)

I done told you, babe,
 —it's understood
You got the best pie in
 this neighborhood.

(*Custard Pie*—Sonny Terry)

He boiled my cabbage
And he made it awful hot.
Then he put the bacon in
And overflowed the pot.

(*Empty Bed Blues*—Traditional)

He's a deep-sea diver
With a stroke that can't go wrong.
He can reach the bottom
'Cause his breath holds out so long.

(*Empty Bed Blues*—Traditional)

Here comes my baby,
Flashin' her new gold tooth.
Well, she's so small
She can mambo in a pay phone booth.

(*Flip, Flop And Fly*—Charles Calhoun/
Lou Willie Turner)

Well, I'm a king bee, baby.
Can buzz all night long.
Yeah, I can buzz better, baby,
When your man is gone.

(*I'm A King Bee*—James H. Moore)

I'm your ice cream man,
Stop me when I'm passing by.
I'll cool you off, little girl,
I guarantee I'll satisfy.

(*Ice Cream Man*—John Brim)

My piston ain't sound—
My mojo is frail.
But when I rub my root,
My luck will never fail.

(*My John The Conquer Root*—Willie Dixon)

Now I can do a rumba,
    and I can do a samba, too;
But a girl like this,
    she don't ever get through.
She's got my knee bones achin',
    she's got my shoulders sore.
When I have done my best,
    she still cries out for more.

(*One More Time*—Willie Dixon)

Rock me baby,
Rock me all night long.
I want you to rock me baby
Like my back ain't got no bone.

(*Rock Me Baby*—B.B. King/Joe Bihari)

Blacker than midnight,
Teeth like flags of truce.
The blacker the berry—
The sweeter is the juice.

(*St. Louis Blues*—W.C. Handy)

When you get enough hot dog,
Stop and rest a while.
If you want any more,
Sam will serve you with a smile.

(*Sam-The Hot Dog Man*—Traditional)

I'm like a one-eyed cat
Peepin' in a seafood store.
Well, I can look at you
'Til you ain't no child no more.

(*Shake, Rattle And Roll*—Charles Calhoun)

It could be a spoonful of diamonds,
It could be a spoonful of gold,
Just a little spoon of your
    precious love
Can satisfy my soul.

(*Spoonful*—Willie Dixon)

I've got a sweet little angel,
I love the way she spreads
    her wings.
Yes, when she spreads her wings
    around me
I get joy in everything.

(*Sweet Little Angel*—B.B. King/Jules Bihari)

The mighty wolf's makin' a
    midnight creep,
The hunters, they can't find him.
Stealin' sheep everywhere he goes,
And draggin' his tail behind him.

(*Tail Dragger*—Willie Dixon)

I was in my bed a-sleepin',
Oh boy, what a dream.
I was dreamin' 'bout my T.V. Mama,
The one with the big, wide screen.

(*T.V. Mama*—Lou Willie Turner)

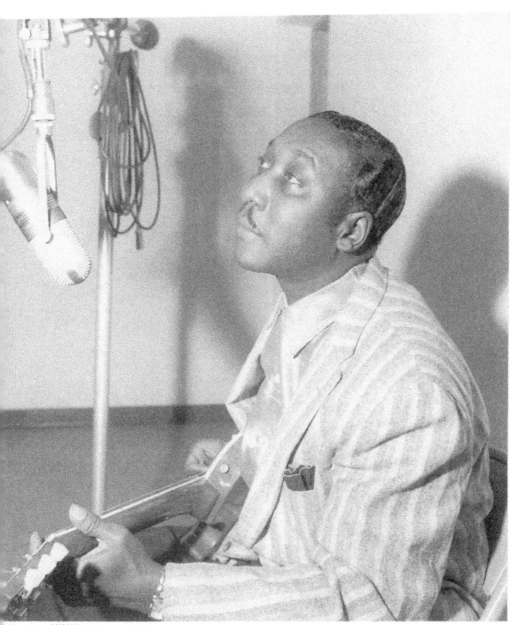

Muddy Waters

Driving Home More Double Entendres

Driving Home More Double Entendres

Although food ranks as **the number** one **sexual** euphemism of choice, vehicles of all kinds seem to work best when describing one's, shall we say, machinery. Chuck Berry took the medium to new heights through a series of songs: "Maybellene," "You Can't Catch Me," "I Want To Be Your Driver" and "No Particular Place To Go" all qualify as songs about much more than just driving around.

If he had sung them a little slower, they would all be considered blues standards today. But, since most pop musicologists define the songs of Chuck Berry as belonging to the rock and roll genre, I've included only the one with the best punchline here.

Of course, the vehicle in question doesn't always have to be a car. Buses and rockets qualify, too.

My baby, she run off with the
    bus driver,
And you know that don't seem right.
Well, he used to give her a lot of
    rides in the daytime,
And now she gives him rides at night.

(*Bus Driver*—McKinley Morganfield
[Muddy Waters]/Terry Abrahamson)

Your motor's put-tin' and poppin'
    and missin' too.
Only one thing left for you to do:
If you give it a push and your
    car don't crank,
I wanna put a tiger in your tank.

(*I Wanna Put A Tiger In Your Tank*
—Willie Dixon)

Wanna let my chauffeur
Drive me around the world.
Then he can be my little boy,
Yes, I'll be his girl.

(*Me And My Chauffeur Blues*—Ernest Lawler)

No particular place to go,
So we parked way out on the cocamo.
The night was young
   and the moon was gold,
So we both decided to take a stroll.
Can you imagine the way I felt?
I couldn't unfasten her safety belt.

(*No Particular Place To Go*—Chuck Berry)

We'll zip it, we'll dip it—
We'll rip it, we'll tip it—
We'll flip it, we'll whip it—
We'll ride and glide
   and be so satisfied.
The trip will be fine
   in my Rocket 69.

(*Rocket 69*—Henry Glover/Lois Mann)

Well, she don't care if I'm stoned
   or sloppy drunk,
Long as she's got the keys
And there's a spare wheel
   in her trunk.

(*She Loves My Automobile*—Billy F Gibbons/
Dusty Hill/Frank Beard)

I flash your lights, mama,
Your horn won't even blow.
Got a short in this connection,
Hoo-well babe, it's way down below.

(*Terraplane Blues*—Robert Johnson)

I'm gonna get down
    in this connection,
Keep on tanglin'
    with your wires,
And when I mash down
    on your little starter,
Then your spark plug
    will give me fire.

(*Terraplane Blues*—Robert Johnson)

Oh, baby—you should take care of
   your little automobile.
Now, you've got a pretty little car,
   baby,
But you let too many get to the wheel.

(*Too Many Drivers*—Big Bill Broonzy)

Bessie Smith

Birth

Birth

According to psychologists, birth is one of the
most traumatic experiences we endure. For blues singers,
birth seems to be split into two major camps: those who
were born unlucky, and those who started bragging the
moment they came out of the womb.

Brownie McGhee sang about being born on Friday the
13th, while Willie Dixon boasted about being "born for
good luck." In "Born Under A Bad Sign," Albert King
sang that he had been down since he began crawl, whereas
the protagonist of Leiber & Stoller's "Trouble" was "born
standing up and talking back."

Blues great J.B. Lenoir took a completely different
approach. One of the most outspoken singer/songwriters
on the subject of disenfranchised African Americans,
Lenoir chose to use death as a metaphor for the birth of
black children in Mississippi.

And, in a song that inspired the name of one of rock and
roll's greatest bands, as well as the name of a popular music
magazine, Muddy Waters was born to be a "Rollin' Stone."

Well, this is a story,
A story ain't never been told.
You know the Blues got pregnant
And they named the baby
   Rock and Roll.

(*The Blues Had A Baby And They Named It
Rock And Roll*—McKinley Morganfield
[Muddy Waters]/Brownie McGhee)

Why was I born in Mississippi
When it's so hard to get ahead?
Every black child
   born in Mississippi,
You know the poor child is born dead.

(*Born Dead*—J.B. Lenoir)

Thirteen children in my family,
I was the last one born.
I was born on bad luck Friday,
Lord, on the thirteenth morn.

(*Born For Bad Luck*—Brownie McGhee)

Some folks were meant to
   live in clover,
But they are such a chosen few.
And clover, being green,
Is something I've never seen
'Cause I was born to be blue.

(*Born To Be Blue*—Robert Wells/Mel Torme)

Born under a bad sign,
I've been down since I began to crawl.
If it wasn't for bad luck,
I wouldn't have no luck at all.

   (*Born Under A Bad Sign*—Booker T. Jones/
   William Bell)

My heart is sad and I'm all forlorn,
My man treats me mean.
I regret the day that I was born
And that man, I ever seen.

   (*A Good Man Is Hard To Find*—Eddie Green)

On the seventh hour,
On the seventh day,
On the seventh month,
The seventh doctor say:
"He was born for good luck,
And that you'll see."
I've got seven hundred dollars,
So don't you mess with me.

([*I'm Your*] *Hoochie Coochie Man*—Willie Dixon)

Well, my mother told my father
Just before I was born,
"I got a boy child comin',
Gonna be a rollin' stone."

(*Rollin' Stone*—McKinley Morganfield
[Muddy Waters])

I was born in a dump,
Mama died and daddy got drunk.
Left me here to die or grow
In the middle of Tobacco Road.

(*Tobacco Road*—John D. Loudermilk)

I was born standin' up
  and talkin' back.
My daddy was a green-eyed
  mountain jack.

(*Trouble*—Jerry Leiber/Mike Stoller)

(Photo by Tom Copi/Frank Driggs Collection)

Albert King

Death

Death

There are a lot of good jokes about musicians, but here's my all-time favorite—Question: What's the epitaph on a blues singer's tombstone? Answer: "*Didn't wake up this morning.*"

Blues songs cover an infinite number of topics, but there's hardly a bluesier subject one can sing about than death. There seems to be only a handful of blues songs about being born, but one would be pretty hard-pressed to find a bluesman who doesn't have at least one song about dying in his repertoire.

In the blues, you either feel like you're *fixing* to die, feel like you *want* to die, feel like you want someone *else* to die, feel like someone wants *you* dead, wish you *were* dead or wish your *lover* were dead.

Of course, if you do kill someone and get caught, you're going to end up behind bars. And, as we'll see in a later chapter, that's another subject that blues singers have a lot to say about.

I'm telling you, baby,
Don't you understand?
I'd rather see you dead, little girl,
Than to be with another man.

(*Baby, Let's Play House*—Arthur Gunter)

I've been your slave
Ever since I've been your babe.
But before I'd be your dog
I'd see you in your grave.

(*Billie's Blues*—Billie Holiday)

Well, I hope you'll see me
When I come streakin' by.
She's got a bad old man,
And I'm too young to die.

(*Down In The Bottom*—Willie Dixon)

Everybody wants to laugh
But nobody wants to cry.
Everybody wants to go to heaven
But nobody wants to die.

(*Everybody Wants To Go To Heaven*—Don Nix)

Please, Ida Belle,
Don't cry this time.
If you'll cry about a nickel
You'll die about a dime.

(*Last Fair Deal Gone Down*—Robert Johnson)

I'm gonna buy myself
A graveyard of my own.
I'm gonna bury that woman
If she don't let me alone.

(*Pinetop's Blues*—Pinetop Smith)

If you'll let me be your slave,
Your love I'll cherish to my grave.
And if you should die before I do,
I'll end my life to be with you.

(*Please Accept My Love*—B.B. King/Sam Ling)

Well, you're so beautiful,
But you've got to die someday.
All I want's a little loving
Just before you pass away.

(*Roll 'Em Pete*—Pete Johnson/Joe Turner)

I said to papa,
    "Can you stand to see me cry?"
He said,
    "Gal, I can stand to see you die."

(*You Don't Know My Mind*—Virginia Liston/
Samuel Gray/Clarence Williams)

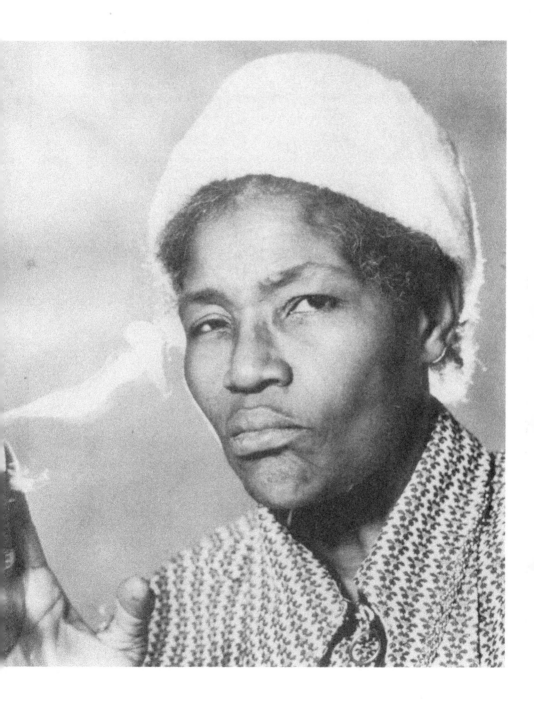

The Birds
& the Bees,
the Dogs
& the Ducks, etc.

The Birds & the Bees, the Dogs & the Ducks, etc.

Blues songs are often filled with metaphors.
For instance, when Slim Harpo sings about his sexual prowess, he doesn't say that he's like a king bee—he claims that he *is* a king bee.

Then there's Willie Mae "Big Mama" Thornton's classic recording of the Leiber & Stoller song "Hound Dog." According to lyricist Jerry Leiber, he was looking for a phrase to replace a familiar obscenity that begins with the adjective "mother." You have to wonder where Elvis would have been today if Leiber had decided not to go with the dog metaphor.

In the simile department, it hardly matters if your dog "can see like an owl" when it's grown so used to the man having an affair with your woman that it doesn't even bark when the guy's in your house.

Whether it's a lyric about a literal blood hound searching for Freddie King's woman, or a tale sung by Lightnin' Slim about an interesting conversation between a pink alligator and an old crocodile, the blues farm is filled with all sorts of animals, insects and other creatures.

Oh, I done got wise to you, baby.
You're not the only bird in the sky.
So don't ask me no questions now, baby,
And I won't tell you no lie.

(*Ask Me No Questions*—B.B. King)

Now, my mama killed a chicken—
   she thought it was a duck.
She put him on the table
   with his legs stickin' up.

(*Bottle It Up And Go*—Robert Brown)

She said, "Take me up, hawky,
Take me up in the sky.
I'm just a little bitty chicken
And I don't know how to fly."

(*The Chicken And The Hawk*—Jerry Leiber/
Mike Stoller)

You ain't nothin' but a hound dog,
Quit snoopin' 'round my door.
You can wag your tail
But I ain't gonna feed you no more.

(*Hound Dog*—Jerry Leiber/Mike Stoller)

The Birds & the Bees, the Dogs & the Ducks, etc.

If you see my little red rooster,
Please drive him home.
There's been no peace
   in the barnyard
Since the little red rooster's
   been gone.

(*Little Red Rooster*—Willie Dixon)

I'm gonna find you, baby,
If it takes my whole life
   to track you down.
If I don't find you by plane,
I'm gonna use my old blood hound.

(*Lonesome Whistle Blues*—Alan Moore/
Elson Teat/Rudy Toombs)

Now he can see like an owl.
He can hear you drop a pin.
But what I'd like to know is
How the hell did you get in?

(*My Dog*—Mickey Baker/Pete Chatman)

Well, if the river was whiskey
And I was a diving duck,
Well, I would dive to the bottom
And never would I come up.

(*Rollin' And Tumblin'*—McKinley Morganfield
[Muddy Waters])

Well the pink alligator told
    the old crocodile,
"Just hang around baby,
    I'm gonna kiss you after 'while."
The crocodile said
    to the pink alligator,
"You got to kiss me now, dad,
    and I'll hang around later."

(*Rooster Blues*—Jerry West)

You can't judge an apple by
    lookin' at the tree.
You can't judge honey by
    lookin' at the bee.
You can't judge a daughter by
    lookin' at the mother.
You can't judge a book by
    lookin' at the cover.

(*You Can't Judge A Book By The Cover*
—Willie Dixon)

Willie Dixon

Bragging Rights

Bragging Rights

Among the many blues songwriters who have shown a special talent for expounding upon their virtues and prowess, the undisputed champion of championing his own cause was the great Willie Dixon.

A staff writer for the primarily blues-based Chess Records in Chicago, Dixon's songs were recorded not only by such Chess acts as Muddy Waters, Howlin' Wolf, Koko Taylor, Little Walter, Bo Diddley and Sonny Boy Williamson, but also by modern bluesmen like Stevie Ray Vaughan, Robert Cray, and Eric Clapton—as well as by classic rock acts including the Rolling Stones, the Allman Brothers Band, Led Zeppelin and ZZ Top.

His songwriting was so prolific and profound that he is reputed to be the most covered blues songwriter of all time. There are a few other songwriters whose lines appear in this chapter on bragging rights, but the vast majority of great blues songs in which the performer literally sings his own praises came from the pen of the man who proudly proclaimed himself to be "300 pounds of heavenly joy."

I *am* a back door man,
Well, the men don't know,
But the little girls understand.

(*Back Door Man*—Willie Dixon)

I'm built for comfort,
I ain't built for speed.
But I got everything
All you good women need.

(*Built For Comfort*—Willie Dixon)

You need grits—go to the grocer's.
You need fish—go to the sea.
You need love—don't go no further.
Just come on home to me.

(*Don't Go No Further*—Willie Dixon)

I got an ax handle pistol
   on a graveyard frame
That shoots tombstone bullets
   wearin' balls and chains.
I'm drinkin' T.N.T.,
   I'm smokin' dynamite.
I hope some screwball starts a fight—
'Cause I'm ready,
Ready as any man can be.
I am ready for you—
I hope you're ready for me.

(*I'm Ready*—Willie Dixon)

Now, when I was a young boy,
At the age of five,
My mother said I'd be
The greatest man alive!

(*Mannish Boy*—McKinley Morganfield
[Muddy Waters]/M.R. London/Ellas McDaniel)

I can heal the sick,
Raise the dead,
And make little girls
Talk out of their heads.

(*The Seventh Son*—Willie Dixon)

Little girl if you take it easy,
Let me make you understand.
You ain't nothing but a female,
And God knows I'm a man.

(*Take It Easy Baby*—Sonny Boy Williamson)

Hoy, hoy, I'm your boy.
I've got three hundred pounds
    of heavenly joy.

(*Three Hundred Pounds Of Joy*—Willie Dixon)

If you're lookin' for trouble,
You came to the right place.
If you're lookin' for trouble,
Just look right in my face.

(*Trouble*—Jerry Leiber/Mike Stoller)

Johnny Winter

Blues for
Christmas

Blues for Christmas

For a **lot of folks—both young and old—Christmas** is the most wonderful time of the year. But when it comes to Christmas blues songs, even December 25th can be a very melancholy day indeed.

While the rest of the world is singing about being home for the holidays, many a Christmas blues song tells the sad story of a lover being gone. The saddest blues singers of the bunch don't even have a Christmas tree on which to hang their balls.

On the other hand, in the case of a different variety of Christmas blues song, we learn that Santa's job is to bring his gifts to some very grown-up girls.

Happily, even a bluesman can sometimes enjoy the holiday season—especially when his woman agrees to hang up her stockings and turn off the lights.

I ain't like old St. Nick,
He don't come but once a year.
But, I'll come running
   with my presents
Every time you call me, dear.

(*Back Door Santa*—Clarence Carter/
Marcus Daniel)

Well, Santa Claus, Mr. Santa Claus,
Oh, listen to my plea.
Don't bring me nothin' for Christmas
   but a brand new Cadillac,
And my baby back home to me.

(*Christmas Blues*—D. Moore)

Santa, oh Santa,
Bring me a full-grown man.
If you ain't got a good one,
Santa, do the best you can.

(*Christmas Man Blues*—unknown)

I hear sleigh bells ringing,
But I haven't heard a word
   from you in years.
Oh, I hear a choir singing,
And I'm just sitting here
   crying Christmas tears.

(*Christmas Tears*—Sonny Thompson/
Robert C. Wilson)

It's Christmas time everybody
But it won't be Christmas for me.
I haven't got my baby,
I don't even have a Christmas tree.

(*Christmas Time For Everyone But Me*
—Hank Ballard)

It's Christmas time,
And I ain't gonna let you
   see my Santa Claus.
You done wore out your undershirt
And you know you ain't
   got no drawers.

(*I Ain't Gonna Let You See My Santa Claus*
—Victoria Spivey)

Merry Christmas, little baby,
You sure been good to me.
I haven't had a drink this mornin'
But I'm all lit up like a
 Christmas tree.

(*Merry Christmas, Baby*—Lou Baxter/
Johnny Moore)

Then won't you tell me
 you'll never more roam?
Christmas and New Year's
 will find you home.
There'll be no more sorrow,
 no grief and pain,
'Cause I'll be happy,
 happy once again.

(*Please Come Home For Christmas*
—Charles Brown/Gene Redd)

Hang up your pretty stockings—
Turn off the light—
Santa Claus is comin'
Down your chimney tonight!

(*Santa Claus Is Back In Town*—Jerry Leiber/
Mike Stoller)

Billie Holiday

Mornings &
Evenings

Mornings & Evenings

As B.B. King said, "The blues is a feeling."
A key element of the blues is the singer's ability to elicit emotions from the listener by creating a mood—a mood shaped not only by the singer's delivery, but also by the song's setting.

In many cases, the brighter the setting, the cheerier the song. For example, pop tunes such as "Good Day Sunshine," "California Sun," and "Great Balls of Fire" all conjure up good feelings of good times.

Blues songs, on the other hand, tend to be at their most somber just prior to dawn ("Blues Before Sunrise") or just after the sun has set ("Evenin'").

But every once in a while, there's an exception to the rule. It's hard not to smile when Sonny Boy Williamson sings, "Good morning, little schoolgirl. Can I go home with you?"

I had the blues before sunrise
With tears standing in my eyes.
It's such a miserable feeling,
A feeling that I feel despised.

(*Blues Before Sunrise*—Leroy Carr)

Can't you hear me talkin' to you,
　baby?
If you can't you better get you a
　hearin' aid.
I got real bad news for you
　this evenin':
Baby, there's gotta be some
　changes made.

(*Can't You Hear Me Talking To You?*
—B.B. King/Dave Clark)

Early in the mornin'
And I ain't got nothin'
  but the blues.

    (*Early In The Mornin'*—Leo Hickman/
    Louis Jordan/Dallas Bartley)

Evenin', every night you come
  and you find me,
And you always come and remind me
That my baby's gone.
Evenin', can't you see I'm deeply
  in your power,
Every minute seems like an hour
Since my gal,
She's gone,
My baby's gone.

    (*Evenin'*—Mitchell Parish/Harry A. White)

I got up this morning,
Blues walkin' 'round my bed.
Went to eat my breakfast,
Blues was all in my bread.

(*Good Mornin' Blues*—Huddie Ledbetter/
Alan Lomax)

Good morning heartache,
You old gloomy sight.
Good morning heartache,
I thought we said goodbye
   last night.

(*Good Morning Heartache*—Dan Fisher/
Irene Higginbotham/Ervin Drake)

Good morning, little schoolgirl.
Can I go home with you?
Tell your mother and your father
I once was a schoolboy, too.

(*Good Morning Little Schoolgirl*
—Sonny Boy Williamson)

I woke up this mornin',
Looked through my window pane.
I was thinkin' about my baby,
But all I saw was rain.

(*Rain Is Such A Lonesome Sound*
—Jimmy Witherspoon/Rachel Witherspoon)

Now here it is, three o'clock
    in the morning,
And I can't even close my eyes.
Well, you know, I can't find my baby,
Pretty girl, I can't be satisfied.

(*Three O'Clock Blues*—B.B. King/Jules Bihari)

Ma Rainey

Nights & Days

Nights & Days

According to **T-Bone Walker, the blues are** at their worst Monday through Thursday. On the other hand, Peter Chatman (a/k/a Memphis Slim) had the blues every day of the week.

Little Willie John saw things in a more positive light—literally. For him, whether there was sunlight or moonlight outside, he always lit up when his woman called his name.

Morning or evening, day or night, the blues are always around.

Today has been a long, long
   lonesome day.
I've been sittin' here thinkin'
With my mind a million miles away.

(*Blues Before Sunrise*—Leroy Carr)

When my days are long and dreary
   and the sun refuses to shine,
I would never be blue and lonely
   if I knew that you were mine.
That's the truth baby; you can
   make everything all right.
Can I see you today, baby, or will
   it have to be tomorrow night?

(*Confessin' The Blues*
—Jay McShann/Walter Brown)

Everyday,
Everyday I have the blues.
When you see me worryin', woman,
Honey, it's you I hate to lose.

(*Everyday [I Have The Blues]*—Peter Chatman)

Sun lights up the daytime,
Moon lights up the night.
I light up when you call my name,
And you know I'm gonna
    treat you right.

(*Fever*—John Davenport/Eddie Cooley)

Forty days and forty nights
Since my baby left this town.
Sun shinin' all day long,
But the rain keeps fallin' down.

(*Forty Days And Forty Nights*—Bernard Roth)

When the evening sun goes down
You will find me hangin' 'round.
The night life ain't no good life,
But it's my life.

(*Night Life*—Willie Nelson/Walt Breeland/
Paul Buskirk)

You know the night time
Is the right time
To be with the one you love.

([*Night Time Is*] *The Right Time*
—Lew Herman/Ozzie Cadena/Napoleon Brown)

See See Rider,
Where did you stay last night?
Your shoes ain't buttoned—
Your clothes don't fit you right.

(*See See Rider*—Ma Rainey/David Eric Rowberry)

They call it Stormy Monday,
But Tuesday's just as bad.
Wednesday's worse,
And Thursday's also sad.

([*They Call It*] *Stormy Monday*—T-Bone Walker)

If I go to church on Sunday,
Then the Cabaret on Monday,
Tain't nobody's biz-ness if I do.

(*Tain't Nobody's Biz-ness If I Do*
—Porter Grainger/Everett Robbins)

It is three hours past midnight
And my baby's nowhere around.
Well, I listen so hard to hear
   her footsteps,
And I ain't even heard a sound.

> (*Three Hours Past Midnight*
> —Johnny Watson/Sam Ling)

The night was black
   and the night was blue,
And around the corner
   an ice wagon flew.
A bump was hit
   and somebody screamed—
You should have heard
   just what I seen.

> (*Who Do You Love?*—Ellas McDaniel)

Jimmy Reed

The Blues
Politic

The Blues Politic

Anyone thinking that protest songs started with
Bob Dylan is a few hundred years too late. Woody Guthrie,
Pete Seeger and the rest of the folk singers of the last half-
century or so were on a bandwagon that's been around
since folks first started singing.

Black field hands in the Mississippi delta and prisoners on
chain gangs in the South of the 1920s and '30s weren't
always singing about "goin' to see Miss Liza." They were
frequently singing protest songs with lines like "The black
folks make the cotton and the white folks get the money."

You don't get the blues unless there's something to be blue
about, and the conditions for African Americans from the
time of the slave ships forward have frequently been cause
for protest.

From the bluntness of Huddie Ledbetter to the eloquence of
Big Bill Broonzy, the blues are perhaps at their most
poignant and potent when used to describe genuine hard-
ship and suffering.

Big boss man,
Can't you hear me when I call?
Well, you ain't so big.
You're just tall—that's all.

(*Big Boss Man*—Luther Dixon/Al Smith)

How many heartaches?
How many years of pain?
Just how many more funerals
Before the streets are safe again?

(*Big City*—Luther Allison/James Solberg)

These white folks in Washington,
They know how
To chuck a colored man a nickel
Just to see him bow.

(*Bourgeois Blues*—Huddie Ledbetter/Alan Lomax)

My money's gone,
My fun is gone.
The way things look,
How can I be here long?

(*Eisenhower Blues*—J.B. Lenoir)

I dreamed I was in the White House,
Settin' in the President's chair.
I dreamed he's shaking my hand,
And he said, "Bill, I'm so glad
    you're here."
But that was just a dream, Lord,
What a dream I had on my mind.
Now, and when I woke up, baby,
Not a chair there could I find.

(*Just A Dream*—Big Bill Broonzy)

What you gonna do
When the welfare turns its back
    on you?
You'll be standin' there stranded.
There ain't a thing that you can do.

(*[The Welfare] Turns Its Back On You*
—Sonny Thompson/Lucious Weaver)

Our Father, who art in heaven,
The white man owes me ten dollars
But I didn't get but seven.
Thy kingdom come, Thy will be done,
I took that or I wouldn't't've got none.

(*That White Mule Of Sin*—John Byrd)

When I first got the blues,
They brought me over on a ship.
Men were standing over me,
And a lot more with a whip.

(*Why I Sing The Blues*—B.B. King/Dave Clark)

I've laid in the ghetto flats,
Cold and numb.
I heard the rats tell the bedbugs
To give the roaches some.

(*Why I Sing The Blues*—B.B. King/Dave Clark)

Sonny Boy
Williamson

Mo' Money/
Mo' Bettin'
Blues

Mo' Money/Mo' Bettin' Blues

The universality of the blues really hits home when it comes to money. Except for the trust fund offspring, generating income is one of life's primary necessities.

All of us need cash, but many of us can also find a way to lose it quickly if a pair of dice, a slot machine, a roulette wheel or a deck of cards is added to the equation.

As is the case with many other subjects in the blues world, gambling can be used as a metaphor. One of the finest examples is the B.B. King/Johnny Pate classic, "Gambler's Blues."

When the subject matter is green, at one time or another, just about everyone has had the blues.

The eagle on the dollar says,
  "In God We Trust."
Woman wants a man—she wants to see
  that dollar first.

(*Hesitation Blues*—Billy Smythe/
J. Scott Middleton)

If I ever get my hands on a
  dollar bill again,
I'm gonna hold on to it
  'til the eagle grins.

(*Nobody Knows You When You're Down And Out*
—Jimmie Cox)

You must be crazy, baby.
You just got to be out of your mind.
As long as I'm footin' the bills,
   woman,
I'm paying the cost to be the boss.

(*Paying The Cost To Be The Boss*—B.B. King)

I asked my baby for a nickel,
And she gave me a
   twenty-dollar bill.
I asked her for a little
   drink of liquor,
And she gave me a whiskey still.

(*Sweet Little Angel*—B.B. King/Jules Bihari)

I said, "I could make you love me,
   darlin',
Baby, I just bet I could."
She says, "Lay your money down,
   babe,
And make your bettin' good."

(*Chicago Blues*—Lonnie Johnson)

Took me a long time,
A long time to find out my mistake.
But I'll bet you my bottom dollar
I'm not fattening no more
   frogs for snakes.

(*Fattening Frogs For Snakes*
—Sonny Boy Williamson)

Well, I don't claim to be no gambler,
    people.
Well, I don't know much about the dice.
Oh, but I wager my baby knows
I'm not the kind that's gonna
    crap out twice.

(*Gambler's Blues*—B.B. King/Johnny Pate)

You upset me baby,
And I don't need nobody else.
I know I'm playing a losing hand,
But I just can't help myself.

(*Losing Hand*—Milton Campbell/Oliver Sain, Jr.)

Buddy Guy

Blues & Booze

Blues & Booze

In the words of that great blues singer Dean Martin, "You're not drunk if you can lie on the floor without holding on."

Alcohol has been prime subject matter for music of every genre. Although country music probably holds the all-time record for most songs about drinking, blues singers have quite a lot to say about the topic as well.

Blues songs about drinking tend to be celebrations, confessionals or the cause for the opposite sex acting the way they do. In songs such as "Saint James Infirmary," the lyrics can pack a lot of pathos. On the other hand, Stick McGhee's "Drinkin' Wine Spo-Dee-O-Dee" is a joyous salute to the numerous choices available from various fruits of the vine.

My buddy had a party,
The cats was on the loose.
We started out with soda
And ended up on juice.

(*Bad Bad Whiskey*—Thomas Davis)

Better stop that drinking
Before it goes to your head.
Wake up some morning,
Find your own self dead.

(*Bad Liquor Blues*—Scrapper Blackwell)

I'm takin' you to the doctor darlin',
Maybe the doctor knows what's
    going on in your head.
You're gonna keep on drinkin' that
    bad wine baby,
Even the grass that grows on your
    grave will be cherry red.

(*Cherry Red Wine*—Luther Allison)

Wine, Wine, Wine - Elderberry
Wine, Wine, Wine - Oh Sherry
Wine, Wine, Wine - Blackberry
Wine, Wine, Wine - Half and Half
Wine, Wine, Wine - Oh Boy
Pass that bottle to me!

(*Drinkin' Wine Spo-Dee-O-Dee*
—Stick McGhee/J. Mayo Williams)

One more nip
And make it strong.
I got to find my baby
If it takes all night long.

(*One Scotch, One Bourbon, One Beer*
—Rudolph Toombs)

I got drunk last night, folks,
Talkin' all out of my head.
It wouldn't have been so bad,
But my baby heard every word I said.

(*Pigmeat And Whiskey Blues*—Traditional)

I went down to old Joe's bar room
On the corner of the square;
They were servin' the drinks as usual
And the usual crowd was there.

(*Saint James Infirmary*—Joe Primrose)

I saw you last evenin'
Standin' up against a tree.
I heard you say you were sick,
But you looked sloppy drunk to me.

(*Sloppy Drunk*—Walter Brown/Jay McShann)

Have mercy!
Been waitin' on the bus all day.
I got my brown paper bag
And my take-home pay.

(*Waitin' For The Bus*—Billy F Gibbons/
Dusty Hill)

John **Lee** Hooker

Guns, Knives, Razors & a Two-by-Four

Guns, Knives, Razors & a Two-by-Four

One of the prime components running throughout the blues is the frankness with which the songs' stories are told. If the singer is sad, you know he's sad. In fact, he *tells* you just how sad he is. Blues singers are not known for being subtle. They don't merely drop hints about what their problems might be. They always come right out and tell you.

If they're feeling happy, they express it in lines like, "I'm so glad. I'm so glad/I'm glad, I'm glad, I'm glad." If they're feeling the opposite, they convey that message with lyrics such as "I feel bad, I feel terrible/I'm just as sad as I can be."

It should come as no surprise, then, that when they're in a fighting mood, they convey that message with words of violence.

Apparently, however, blues singers have universally chosen not to bruise their knuckles with fisticuffs. Among the choice of weapons in this chapter are guns, knives, razors and a two-by-four. The only exception to the rule is the George Brooks composition, made famous by Bessie Smith, about a woman who starts off by stabbing her lover with a knife, and then finishes the job by kicking him to death!

Boom, boom, boom, boom—
I'm gonna shoot you right down.

(*Boom Boom*—John Lee Hooker)

I wore my forty-four so long
I done made my shoulder sore.
Well, I'm wonderin', everybody,
Where'd my baby go?

(*Forty-Four*—Chester Burnett)

I don't want him
To be riding these girls around.
So I'm gonna steal me a pistol,
Shoot my chauffeur down.

(*Me And My Chauffeur Blues*—Ernest Lawler)

You women don't have to worry
'Bout your life.
She made Jack the Ripper
Throw away his knife.

(*No Matter How She Done It*—Tampa Red)

I heard a woman scream,
Yeah, and I peaked through the door.
Some cat was workin' on Annie
Lord, with a two-by-four.

(*Tin Pan Alley*—Robert Geddins)

I cut him with my Barlow,
I kicked him in the thigh.
I stood there laughing over him
While he wallowed 'round and died.

(*Send Me To The 'Lectric Chair*—George Brooks)

It could be a spoonful of water
Saved from the desert sand.
But one spoon of luck from my
    little forty-five
Can save you from another man.

(*Spoonful*—Willie Dixon)

I'm gonna shoot my pistol,
Gonna shoot my Gatlin' gun.
You made me love you,
Now your man done come.

(*32-20 Blues*—Robert Johnson)

Tell Automatic Slim,
   tell Razor Totin' Jim.
Tell Butcher Knife Totin' Annie,
   tell Fast Talkin' Fannie.
We gonna pitch a ball—
   a-down to the union hall.
We gonna romp and tromp
   'til midnight,
We gonna fuss and fight
   'til daylight.
We gonna pitch a wang dang doodle
   all night long.

   (*Wang Dang Doodle*—Willie Dixon)

Don't bother my baby,
No tellin' what she'd do.
Now that girl may cut you,
She may shoot you, too.

   (*Walking Through The Park*
   —McKinley Morganfield [Muddy Waters])

Howlin' Wolf

Blues
Behind Bars

Blues Behind Bars

The Mississippi State Penitentiary, also known as Parchman Farm, has been the temporary (and sometimes permanent) home to many men, including blues singer Bukka White. One of White's best-known recordings, "Parchman Farm Blues," told the tale of his more than two years spent there.

Although blues singer/pianist Mose Allison didn't serve time in any state pen, he sang about the one in Mississippi in his acerbic "New Parchman."

Huddie "Leadbelly" Ledbetter never landed in Parchman, but he found himself behind bars on several occasions. Remarkably he managed to sing his way out of both the Texas and Louisiana state pens.

And then there's the fictional character Scarface Jones, who attempted a less conventional way to get out of prison.

Many days of sorrow,
Many days of woe,
And a ball and chain—
Everywhere I go.

(*Chain Gang Blues*—Thomas A. Dorsey/
Charles J. Parker)

I know my baby,
She's gonna jump and shout
When the train comes in
And I come walking out.

(*County Jail Blues*—Alfred Fields)

Well, I ain't superstitious,
But a black cat just crossed my trail.
Don't sweep me with no broom,
I might get put in jail.

(*I Ain't Superstitious*—Willie Dixon)

Thirty days in jail
With my back turned to the wall.
Look here, mister jail keeper,
Put another gal in my stall.

(*Jailhouse Blues*—Bessie Smith/
Clarence Williams)

You go to court and I'll come along,
You go to jail, I'll go your bond.
You got time, tell you what I'll do:
I'll stay outside and wait for you.

(*Little Baby [You Go And I'll Go With You]*
—Willie Dixon)

Oh listen you men,
I don't mean no harm.
If you wanna do good,
You better stay off old
   Parchman Farm.

(*Parchman Farm Blues*—Bukka White)

Well, I'm sittin' over here on
   Parchman Farm,
Well, I'm sittin' over here on
   Parchman Farm,
The place is loaded with
   rustic charm.

(*New Parchman*—Mose Allison)

The copper brought her in,
She didn't need no bail.
She shook it for the judge
And put the cop in jail.

(*No Matter How She Done It*—Tampa Red)

The warden said, "Come out with
   your hands up in the air.
If you don't stop this riot,
   you're all gonna get the chair."
Scarface Jones said,
   "It's too late to quit.
Pass the dynamite,
   'cause the fuse is lit."

(*Riot In Cell Block # 9*—Jerry Leiber/Mike Stoller)

I'm in trouble, no one to pay my fine.
When I get out this time,
   gonna leave this town a-flyin'.
I was with my buddy through thick
   and thin.
My buddy got away, and I got in.

(*Sun Gonna Shine In My Door*—Big Bill Broonzy)

Now I don't like this place, mama,
And I never will.
I can sit right here in jail
And look at Vicksburg on the hill.

(*Vicksburg Blues*—Traditional)

Stevie Ray Vaughan

Hmmm,
Sounds Familiar

Hmmm, Sounds Familiar

When it comes to blues melodies, it's safe to say that almost everyone who ever wrote a blues song is guilty of having copied whomever that person was who composed the very first 12-bar blues tune.

Although it's uncommon for anyone to write a wholly new blues melody for the standard I-IV-V chord progression ("Kansas City" being a rare exception to the rule), the subject matter of blues lyrics can vary widely.

Some lyrics—such as those in Stevie Ray Vaughan's "Pride And Joy"—pay tribute to earlier blues standards. On occasion, though, it would appear that a number of Stevie's fellow blues songwriters heard a line or two of lyrics that they liked, and decided that imitation was the finest form of flattery. Now, if only I could copyright the phrase "Woke up this morning. . . ."

The woman I love
Took from my best friend.
Some joker got lucky,
Stole her back again.

(*Come On In My Kitchen*—Robert Johnson)

Well, the girl I love,
I stole her from a friend.
He got lucky,
Stole her back again.

(*Mercury Blues*—K.C. Douglas/Robert Geddins)

Love is like a faucet:
It turns off and on.
Sometimes when you think it's on,
   baby,
It has turned off and gone.

(*Fine And Mellow*—Billie Holiday)

Hey, baby,
Don't throw your love on me
   so strong.
Yeah, your love is like a faucet:
You can turn it off and on.

(*Don't Throw Your Love On Me So Strong*
—Albert King)

You're talkin' about your woman.
I wish to God that you could
   see mine.
Every time the little girl starts
   to lovin'
She brings eyesight to the blind.

(*Eyesight To The Blind*—Sonny Boy Williamson)

Well, you've heard about lovin'
Givin' sight to the blind.
My baby's lovin'
Causes the sun to shine.

(*Pride And Joy*—Stevie Ray Vaughan)

Woke up this morning,
My baby was gone.

(*Woke Up This Morning [My Baby's Gone]*
—B.B. King/Saul Bihari)

I woke up this mornin',
Feelin' 'round for my shoes.

(*Walking Blues*—Robert Johnson)

I woke up this morning
'Bout half past three.

(*Mojo Hand Blues*—Ida Cox)

When I woke up this morning,
All I had was gone.

(*Rollin' And Tumblin'*—McKinley Morganfield
[Muddy Waters])

B.B. King

Love—or the Lack Thereof

Love–or the Lack Thereof

As is the case with every other genre of music
throughout the world, there are more blues songs that
focus on love than on any other topic.

Since we're talking blues, most of the songs are about the
heartache of love gone wrong, the tragedy of unrequited
love, the overwhelming need for love, the jealousy of love
lost to another—you get the picture.

Luckily, every now and then, even in the blues there are
actually songs about being in love. And, not surprisingly,
there are also plenty of songs about making love.

Of all the lines from all the blues songs in existence,
you probably won't come across any more tragic than
B.B. King's sad lament: "Nobody loves me but my mother—
and she could be jivin', too."

Nobody loves me,
Nobody seems to care.
Speakin' of bad luck and trouble,
Well, you know I've had my share.

(*Everyday [I Have The Blues]*—Pete Chatman)

Begged for mercy,
    prayed to my God above,
Somebody please help me,
    send me someone to love.
I'll call the Mod Squad or the F.B.I.
Mm, I need some answers,
    somebody tell me why.

(*I Believe I've Been Blue Too Long*—B.B. King/
Dave Clark)

I don't want you to be no slave,
I don't want you to work all day.
I don't want you to be true,
I just want to make love to you.

(*I Just Want To Make Love To You*—Willie Dixon)

If you ever, ever should leave me,
My world would tumble down,
For you're the key to my kingdom
And your love is my crown.

(*Key To My Kingdom*—Maxwell Davis/
Joe Bihari/Claude Baum)

Take me in your arms
   and never let me go,
Whisper to me softly
   while the moon is low,
Hold me close and tell me
   what I want to know,
Say it to me gently;
   let the sweet talk flow,
Come a little closer—
   make love to me.

(*Make Love To Me*—George Brunies/
Allan Copeland/Paul Mares/Walter Melrose/
Bill Norvas/Benny Pollack/Leon Roppolo/
Mel Stitzel)

Nobody loves me but my mother—
And she could be jivin', too.
Now you see why I act funny, baby,
When you do the things you do.

(*Nobody Loves Me But My Mother*—B.B. King)

Heaven, please send to all mankind
Understanding and peace of mind.
But if it's not asking too much,
Please send me someone to love.

(*Please Send Me Someone To Love*—Percy Mayfield)

My lovin' man's sweet as he can be,
But the dog gone fool
    turned sour on me.

(*Sugar Blues*—Lucy Fletcher/Clarence Williams)

Baby, way down inside,
Woman, you need love.

(*You Need Love*—Willie Dixon)

Now, if you wanna love that woman,
You love her with a thrill.
'Cause if you don't,
Some other man will.

(*You've Got To Love Her With A Feeling*
—Freddie King/Sonny Thompson)

T-Bone Walker

Poetry of
the Blues

Poetry of the Blues

Although many songwriters might wish their words to be considered poetry by critics and the public alike, in reality it's very seldom that a song's lyrics actually rise to the level of works by William Blake, Langston Hughes, Walt Whitman, Maya Angelou, Robert Frost, Emily Dickinson or any of those other poets we were supposed to be reading in high school.

On rare occasion, however, a lyric will come along that is so well crafted, so moving and so eloquent that it transcends being merely words to a song.

While most blues aficionados heap enormous praise on the guitar playing of Delta blues giant Robert Johnson, to me many of his song lyrics were every bit as important as his musical talents. And from time to time, the lines he wrote reached the same pinnacle as those of the aforementioned poets.

Including three of Johnson's best, here are the blues as poetry.

I went down to the crossroad,
Fell down on my knees.
Asked the Lord above,
"Have mercy, now, save poor Bob,
    if you please."

(*Cross Road Blues*—Robert Johnson)

Blues fallin' down like hail
Blues fallin' down like hail
And the day keeps on worryin' me
There's a hell hound on my trail
Hell hound on my trail

(*Hell Hound On My Trail*—Robert Johnson)

When things go wrong,
So wrong with you,
It hurts me too.

(*It Hurts Me Too*—Mel London)

When the train, it left the station
With two lights on behind—
Well, the blue light was my blues
And the red light was my mind.

(*Love In Vain*—Robert Johnson)

Yes, my baby left me,
Never said a word.
Was it something that I done—
Something that she heard?

(*My Baby Left Me*—Arthur Crudup)

The sky is crying.
Look at the tears
   roll down the street.

(*The Sky Is Crying*—Elmore James)

Have your fun while you can,
Fate's an awful thing.
You can't tell what might happen,
That's why I love to sing.

(*T-Bone Shuffle*—T-Bone Walker)

You know I'm free, free now baby.
I'm free from your spell.
And now that it's all over,
All I can do is wish you well.

(*The Thrill Is Gone*—Roy Hawkins/Rick Darnell)

Trouble in mind—I'm blue,
But I won't be blue always,
For the sun will shine
In my back door someday.

(*Trouble In Mind*—Richard M. Jones)

My love was big
Your love was small.
And now I've got
No love at all.

(*Weary Blues*—Mort Greene/
George Cates/Artie Matthews)

Photo by Mick Hutson/Redfern)

Eric Clapton

Time to Go

Time to Go

Some blues singers go away because they're tired of being wherever they are. Others leave because they're being thrown out. Some split in a hurry because they're on the run from the law.

After all, when it's time to go, it's time to go!

I got the key to the highway.
Yes, I'm billed out and bound to go.
I'm gonna leave here runnin'
'Cause walkin's most too slow.

(*Key To The Highway*
—Big Bill Broonzy/Chas. Segar)

I'm leavin' town tomorrow,
Leavin' town for sure.
Then you won't be bothered with me
Hangin' 'round your door.

(*That's All Right*—Arthur Crudup)

My baby she wrote me a letter,
She didn't call me on the phone.
Five little words was all she wrote:
"See ya later, I'm gone."

(*You Can Love Yourself*—Kevin Moore)

Discography

DISCOGRAPHY

If you'd like to hear many of the songs appearing on the previous pages, following is a list of CDs I highly recommend. For the most part, this discography is a listing of the artists' "Greatest Hits," "Best Ofs," and "Anthologies" that are currently in print.

I've left out some of my favorite blues albums either because their lyrics don't appear in this book, or to avoid repetition of some of the songs (although you're going to find that a little repetition has been unavoidable). If you aren't already a blues CD collector, you'll definitely want to expand upon the albums I've listed. I realize that creating any kind of discography is just begging for trouble, so please bear in mind that this list isn't even the sharp edge at the very top of the tip of the iceberg. It's only meant as a starting point.

To dig deeper into the blues, check out www.allmusic.com on the web. Once you're there, click on "blues" and you'll find enough information to turn you into a blues expert in no time. There are also dozens of excellent books on the subject, as well as magazines such as *Living Blues, Blues Revue,* and *Juke Blues.*

Be forewarned, however: Blues music can be very addictive. Make sure you've got plenty of shelf space, because listening to the following CDs can lead to a lifetime of collecting the blues.

The Best Of Mose Allison—Mose Allison (Atlantic Jazz)

    Includes   "New Parchman"
                  "Seventh Son"

At Fillmore East—The Allman Brothers Band
    (PolyGram/Capricorn)

    Includes   "Statesboro Blues" (with alternate lyrics)
                  "Stormy Monday"

Five Long Years—Eddie Boyd (Evidence)

    Includes   "Five Long Years"

That's All Right Mama—Arthur "Big Boy" Crudup
    (Bluebird/RCA)

    Includes   "My Baby Left Me"
                  "That's All Right"

Bo Diddley: His Best—Bo Diddley (MCA/Chess)

    Includes   "Who Do You Love?"
                  "You Can't Judge A Book By Its Cover"

San Francisco Bay Blues—Jesse Fuller (Good Time Jazz)

    Includes   "San Francisco Bay Blues"

Baby, Let's Play House: Best Of Arthur Gunter
    —Arthur Gunter (Excello)

    Includes   "Baby, Let's Play House"

Best Of Slim Harpo—Slim Harpo (Hip-O)
    Includes   "I'm A King Bee"

The Billie Holiday Songbook—Billie Holiday (Verve)
    Includes   "Billie's Blues"
                "Fine And Mellow"
                "Good Morning Heartache"

The Very Best Of John Lee Hooker—John Lee Hooker (Rhino)
    Includes   "Boom Boom"

Howlin' Wolf: His Best—Howlin' Wolf (MCA/Chess)
    Includes   "Back Door Man"
                "Built For Comfort"
                "Forty-Four"
                "I Ain't Superstitious"
                "The Red Rooster"
                    (a/k/a "Little Red Rooster")
                "Spoonful"
                "Three Hundred Pounds Of Joy"

Howlin' Wolf: His Best, Vol. 2—Howlin' Wolf (MCA/Chess)
    Includes   "Down In The Bottom"
                "Tail Dragger"

The Sky Is Crying: The History Of Elmore James—Elmore James (Rhino)
    Includes   "It Hurts Me Too"
                "The Sky Is Crying"

Fever: The Best Of Little Willie John—Little Willie John
(Rhino)
Includes   "Fever"

He's A Jelly Roll Baker—Lonnie Johnson (Bluebird/RCA)
Includes   "Chicago Blues"

King Of The Delta Blues—Robert Johnson
(Columbia/Legacy)
Includes   "Come On In My Kitchen"
            "Cross Road Blues"
            "Hell Hound On My Trail"
            "I Believe I'll Dust My Broom"
            "Kindhearted Woman Blues"
            "Last Fair Deal Gone Down"
            "Love In Vain"
            "Sweet Home Chicago"
            "Terraplane Blues"
            "32-20 Blues"

Lovejoy—Albert King (Stax)
Includes   "Everybody Wants To Go To Heaven"

The Very Best Of Albert King—Albert King (Rhino)
Includes   "Born Under A Bad Sign"
            "Crosscut Saw"
            "Don't Throw Your Love On Me So Strong"

A Christmas Celebration Of Hope—B.B. King (MCA)
> Includes   "Back Door Santa"
> "Merry Christmas Baby"
> "Please Come Home For Christmas"

Completely Well—B.B. King (MCA)
> Includes   "Confessin' The Blues"
> "Key To My Kingdom"
> "The Thrill Is Gone"

Deuces Wild—B.B. King (MCA)
> Includes   "Night Life" performed by
> B.B. King & Willie Nelson

King Of The Blues [Box Set]—B.B. King (MCA)
> Includes   "Ask Me No Questions"
> "Confessin' The Blues"
> "Everyday (I Have The Blues)"
> "Gambler's Blues"
> "Nobody Loves Me But My Mother"
> "Paying the Cost To Be The Boss"
> "Please Accept My Love"
> "Rock Me Baby"
> "Sweet Little Angel"
> "Three O'Clock Blues"
> "The Thrill Is Gone"
> "Why I Sing The Blues"
> "You Upset Me Baby"

Riding With The King—B.B. King & Eric Clapton
  (Reprise)
  Includes   "Key To the Highway"

Ultimate Collection—Freddie King (Hip-O)
  Includes   "I'm Tore Down"
              "Lonesome Whistle Blues"
              "You've Got To Love Her With A Feeling"

Absolutely The Best—Leadbelly (Fuel 2000)
  Includes   "The Bourgeois Blues"

Vietnam Blues—J.B. Lenoir (Evidence)
  Includes   "Born Dead"
              "Tax Payin' Blues"
                (a/k/a "Eisenhower Blues")

Going Back To Kay Cee—Little Willie Littlefield & Friends
  (Ace)
  Includes   "K.C. Lovin'" (a/k/a "Kansas City")

Little Walter: His Best—Little Walter (MCA/Chess)
  Includes   "My Babe"

Poet Of The Blues—Percy Mayfield (Specialty)
  Includes   "Please Send Me Someone To Love"

The Essential—Blind Willie McTell (Classic Blues)
  Includes   "Statesboro Blues"

Just Like You—Keb' Mo' (Okeh/550/Epic)
    Includes   "You Can Love Yourself"

Blues Masters: The Very Best Of Jimmy Reed—Jimmy Reed
    (Rhino)
    Includes   "Big Boss Man"
               "Bright Lights, Big City"

The Empress Of The Blues—Bessie Smith (Prism)
    Includes   "Empty Bed Blues"
               "A Good Man Is Hard To Find"
               "Nobody Knows You When You're
                   Down And Out"
               "Send Me To The 'Lectric Chair"
               "Tain't Nobody's Biz-ness If I Do"

The Guitar Wizard—Tampa Red (Columbia/Legacy)
    Includes   "No Matter How She Done It"

What It Takes: The Chess Years—Koko Taylor
    (MCA/Chess)
    Includes   "Wang Dang Doodle"

Hound Dog: The Peacock Recordings—Big Mama Thornton
    (MCA)
    Includes   "Hound Dog"

The Very Best Of Big Joe Turner—Big Joe Turner (Rhino)

Includes   "The Chicken And The Hawk"
"Flip, Flop And Fly"
"Shake, Rattle And Roll"
"T.V. Mama"

Blue Yule: Christmas Blues And R&B Classics—
Various Artists (Rhino)

Includes   "Christmas Blues"
performed by Canned Heat
"Merry Christmas, Baby"
performed by Charles Brown
"Please Come Home For Christmas"
performed by Insight

Atlantic Blues: Piano—Various Artists (Atlantic)

Includes   "Roll 'Em Pete" performed by Joe Turner

Raunchy Business: Hot Nuts & Lollypops—Various Artists
(Columbia/Legacy)

Includes   "The Best Jockey In Town"
performed by Lonnie Johnson
"Sam–The Hot Dog Man"
performed by Lil Johnson

*Strut That Thing: The Essential Recordings Of Piano Blues
And Boogie*—Various Artists (Indigo)

Includes   "Blues Before Sunrise"
performed by Leroy Carr
"Vicksburg Blues" performed by
Little Brother Montgomery

Couldn't Stand The Weather—Stevie Ray Vaughan And
Double Trouble (Epic/Legacy)
Includes   "Tin Pan Alley"
            (a/k/a "Roughest Place In Town")

Greatest Hits—Stevie Ray Vaughan And Double Trouble
(Sony/Epic)
Includes   "Pride And Joy"

T-Bone Blues—T-Bone Walker (Atlantic)
Includes   "Evenin'"
            "(They Call It) Stormy Monday"
            "T-Bone Shuffle"

The Anthology: 1947–1972—Muddy Waters (MCA/Chess)
Includes   "Don't Go No Further"
            "Forty Days And Forty Nights"
            "Good Morning Little Schoolgirl"
            "Hoochie Coochie Man"
                (a/k/a "[I'm Your] Hoochie Coochie Man")
            "I Just Want To Make Love To You"
            "I'm Ready"
            "Mannish Boy"
            "Rollin' And Tumblin', Part 1"
            "Rollin' Stone"
            "Walking Through The Park"
            "You Need Love"

Folk Singer—Muddy Waters (MCA/Chess)
    Includes   "My John The Conquer Root"

Hard Again—Muddy Waters (Sony/Blue Sky)
    Includes   "The Blues Had A Baby And
                    They Named It Rock And Roll"
           "Bus Driver"

The Complete Bukka White —Bukka White
    (Columbia/Legacy)
    Includes   "Parchman Farm Blues"

The Bluebird Recordings: 1937-1938
    —Sonny Boy Williamson (I) (RCA/Bluebird)
    Includes   "Good Morning Little Schoolgirl"

King Biscuit Time—Sonny Boy Williamson (II)
    (Arhoolie)
    Includes   "Eyesight To The Blind"

Sonny Boy Williamson: His Best—Sonny Boy Williamson (II)
    (MCA/Chess)
    Includes   "Fattening Frogs For Snakes"

Saints & Sinners—Johnny Winter (Columbia)
    Includes   "Riot In Cell Block # 9"

Jazz Me Blues: The Best Of Jimmy Witherspoon
—Jimmy Witherspoon (Prestige)
Includes　"Bad Bad Whiskey"
"One Scotch, One Bourbon, One Beer"
"Tain't Nobody's Biz-ness If I Do"
"Trouble In Mind"
"When The Lights Go Out"

Deguello—ZZ Top (Warner Brothers)
Includes　"She Loves My Automobile"

Greatest Hits—ZZ Top (Warner Brothers)
Includes　"My Head's In Mississippi"

Tres Hombres—ZZ Top (Warner Brothers)
Includes　"Waitin' For The Bus"

INDEX OF SONGS

COPYRIGHT CREDITS

Sun Gonna Shine In My Door; By Big Bill Broonzy (BMI). Copyright © 1947 Universal — Duchess Music Corp. Used by Permission. International Copyright Secured. All Rights Reserved. / **Sweet Home Chicago;** Words and Music by Robert Johnson. Copyright © (1978), 1990, 1991 Lehsem II, LLC and Claud L. Johnson. Administered by Music & Media International, Inc. International Copyright Secured. All Rights Reserved. / **Sweet Little Angel;** By Riley B. King and Jules Bihari. © 1956 Careers-BMG Music Publishing, Inc. (BMI). All rights reserved. Used by permission. / **Tail Dragger;** Written by WILLIE DIXON. © 1964 (Renewed 1992) HOOCHIE COOCHIE MUSIC (BMI). (Administered by BUG MUSIC). All Rights Reserved. Used by Permission. / **Take It Easy Baby;** Words and Music by Sonny Boy Williamson. Copyright © 1966 (Renewed) by Arc Music Corporation (BMI). International Copyright Secured. All Rights Reserved. Used by Permission. / **T-Bone Shuffle;** By T-Bone Walker. Copyright © 1959 by Unichappell Music Inc. Copyright Renewed. International Copyright Secured. All Rights Reserved. / **Terraplane Blues;** Words and Music by Robert Johnson. Copyright © (1978), 1990, 1991 Lehsem II, LLC and Claud L. Johnson. Administered by Music & Media International, Inc. International Copyright Secured. All Rights Reserved. / **(They Call It) Stormy Monday;** Words and Music by Aaron "T-Bone" Walker. Copyright © 1947; Renewed 1975 Gregmark Music, Inc. (BMI). Worldwide Rights excluding the British Reversionary Territories but including Canada for Gregmark Music, Inc. Administered by Cherry River Music Co. International Copyright Secured. All Rights Reserved. / **That's All Right;** Words and Music by Arthur Crudup. Copyright © 1947 by Unichappell Music Inc. and Crudup Music. Copyright Renewed. All Rights Administered by Unichappell Music Inc. International Copyright Secured. All Rights Reserved. / **32-20 Blues;** Words and Music by Robert Johnson. Copyright © (1978), 1990, 1991 Lehsem II, LLC and Claud L. Johnson. Administered by Music & Media International, Inc. International Copyright Secured. All Rights Reserved. / **Three Hours Past Midnight;** By Johnny Watson and Saul "Sam Ling" Bihari. © 1970 Careers-BMG Music Publishing, Inc. (BMI). All rights reserved. Used by permission. / **Three Hundred Pounds Of Joy;** Written by WILLIE DIXON. © 1963 (Renewed 1991) HOOCHIE COOCHIE MUSIC (BMI). (Administered by BUG MUSIC). All Rights Reserved. Used by Permission. / **Three O'Clock Blues;** By Riley B. King and Jules Bihari. © 1952 Careers-BMG Music Publishing, Inc. (BMI). All rights reserved. Used by permission. / **The Thrill Is Gone;** By Roy Hawkins and Rick Darnell. © 1951 Careers-BMG Music Publishing, Inc. (BMI). All rights reserved. Used by permission. /

CPSIA information can be obtained
at www.ICGtesting.com
Printed in the USA
BVHW040849210220
572987BV00012B/289

9 780634 055461